Explore and Draw

AIRPLANES

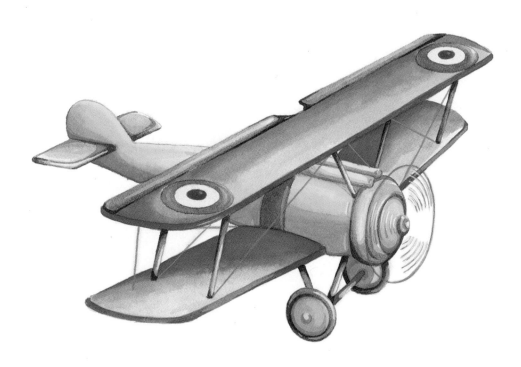

Ann Becker

www.rourkepublishing.com

Editor: Penny Dowdy
Art Direction: Tarang Saggar (Q2AMedia)
Designer: Bhajneek Singh (Q2AMedia)
Picture researcher: Jim Mathew (Q2AMedia)
Picture credits:
t=top b=bottom c=centre l=left r=right

Cover: U.S. Air Force/Staff Sgt. Cherie A. Thurlby.
Insides: Bettmann/Corbis: 4, Popperfoto/Getty Images: 5,
Underwood & Underwood/Corbis: 10,
Museum of Flight/Corbis: 11, Michael Rosa/Shutterstock: 14,
Annedave/Dreamstime: 15, Fizpok/Shutterstock: 19.
Q2AMedia Art Bank: Cover, Title Page, 4, 5, 8, 9, 12, 13, 16, 17, 18, 19, 20, 21, 22.

Library of Congress Cataloging-in-Publication Data

Becker, Ann, 1965 Oct. 6-
Airplanes : explore and draw / Ann Becker.
p. cm. ⁊ (Explore and draw)
Includes index.
ISBN 978-1-60694-355-7 (hard cover)
ISBN 978-1-60694-839-2 (soft cover)
1. Airplanes in art–Juvenile literature. 2. Drawing–Technique–Juvenile literature.
I. Title. II. Title: Explore and draw.
NC825.A4B43 2009
743'.8962913334–dc22
2009021617

Printed in the USA
CG/CG

ROURKE PUBLISHING

www.rourkepublishing.com - rourke@rourkepublishing.com
Post Office Box 643328 Vero Beach, Florida 32964

Contents

Technique

Before you start drawing different kinds of airplanes, let's talk about **perspective**. Using perspective in your drawings will make them look **three-dimensional**. Perspective makes your drawing look less flat.

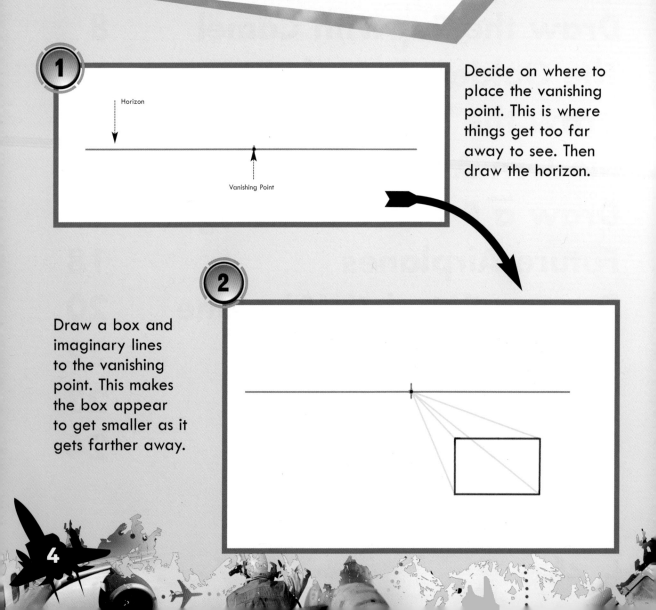

1

Horizon

Vanishing Point

Decide on where to place the vanishing point. This is where things get too far away to see. Then draw the horizon.

2

Draw a box and imaginary lines to the vanishing point. This makes the box appear to get smaller as it gets farther away.

3

Remember that perspective makes drawings look three-dimensional. The rectangle looks big, but appears to get smaller as it gets closer to the vanishing point.

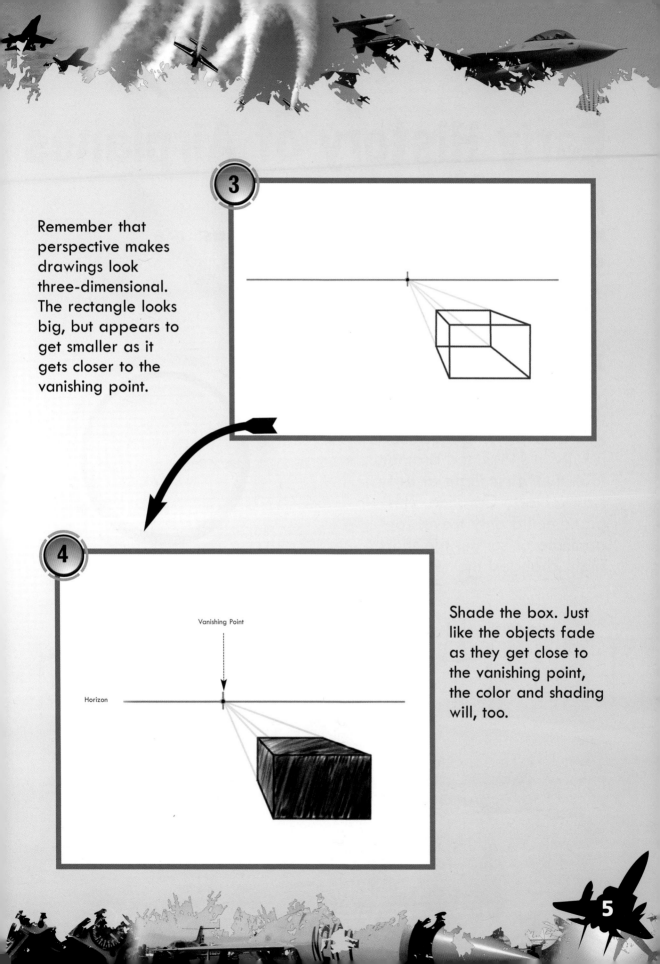

4

Vanishing Point

Horizon

Shade the box. Just like the objects fade as they get close to the vanishing point, the color and shading will, too.

Early History of Airplanes

People have dreamed of flying for thousands of years. But these old ideas didn't come true for a long, long time.

The Wright Time

Wilbur and Orville Wright puzzled for years over how to create a flying machine. Finally in 1903, the brothers took their first flight at Kitty Hawk, North Carolina. This plane could only travel for a minute or so. But the short flight changed the world.

The *Wright Flyer* made its historic flight in Kitty Hawk, NC.

Glenn Curtiss pilots one of his *Golden Flyers*.

Blériot XI

The Wright Brothers were not alone building flying machines. French inventor Louis Blériot started designing airplanes in 1900. He spent eight years and his entire **fortune** building ten airplanes that all crashed. When a newspaper offered a prize to the first person to fly across the **English Channel**, Blériot took the challenge. In 1909, his eleventh plane, the *Blériot XI*, flew across the Channel. He crashed the plane in France but won the contest.

Curtiss *Golden Flyer*

Glenn Curtiss rivaled the Wright Brothers in the U.S. He started selling planes in 1910 in New York. He covered his planes with a golden fabric, which led to the name the *Golden Flyer*.

Airplanes in War

The invention of the airplane came shortly before World War I. Planes became tools of war. Airplanes could carry armed soldiers to attack forces on the ground as well as other planes in the air.

Draw the Sopwith Camel

The Sopwith Camel was the best fighting plane in World War I.

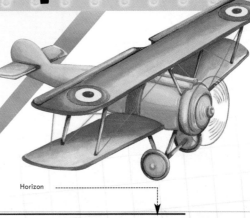

Horizon

Vanishing Point

1 Start with the horizon line and vanishing point. As you draw the body of the plane, the lines should lead to the vanishing point.

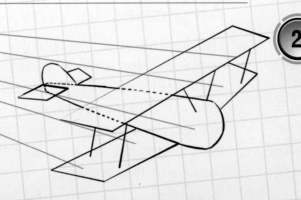

2 Add the wings and tail. The wings should be stacked, one above the other.

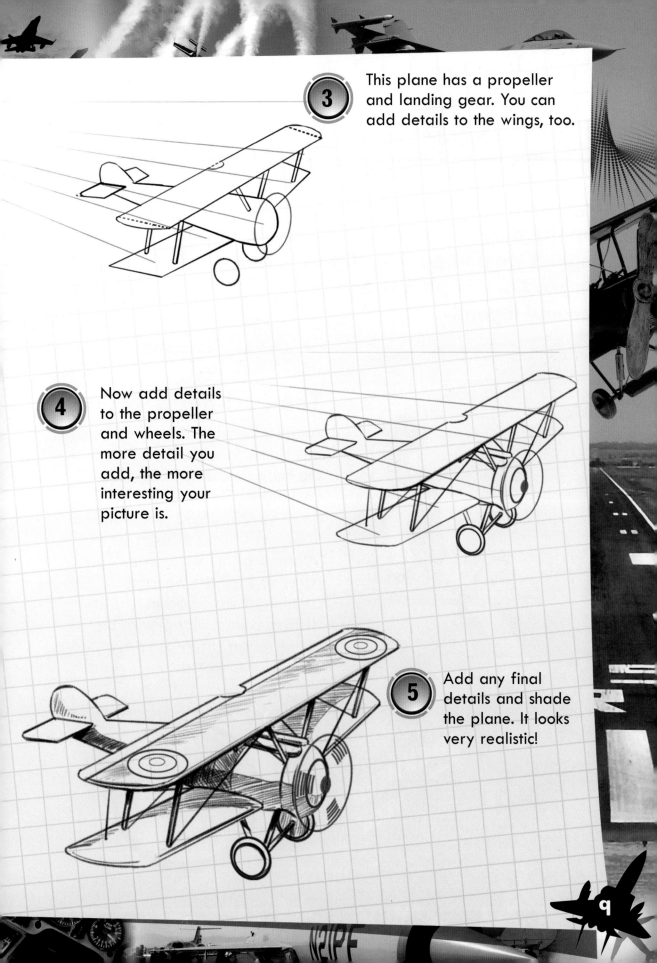

3 This plane has a propeller and landing gear. You can add details to the wings, too.

4 Now add details to the propeller and wheels. The more detail you add, the more interesting your picture is.

5 Add any final details and shade the plane. It looks very realistic!

The Golden Age of Flight

The designs of airplanes changed rapidly during and after World War I. Engines gained power. Flights lasted longer. Certain planes and pilots became legends.

The Lockheed *Vega*

Amelia Earhart flew the Vega, the first plane ever built by the manufacturing company Lockheed. She left Canada on May 20, 1932 and landed in Ireland just 14 hours later. Women pilots were very **rare**, so Earhart became an instant star. Earhart later disappeared along with her plane in an attempt to fly around the world.

Amelia Earhart became a flying legend.

The *Spirit of St. Louis*

In 1919, a rich businessman offered $25,000 to the first person to fly nonstop from New York to Paris. For eight years men failed. Some died trying. In 1927, Charles Lindbergh built a plane in St. Louis, Missouri. He took off in the *Spirit of St. Louis* from New York on May 20, 1927 and landed in Paris 3,312 hours later. The flight was celebrated around the world.

The *China Clipper*

Pilots showed that planes could fly long enough to get across an ocean. It didn't take long for companies to build planes to carry many people across these oceans. The first airplane to take passengers across the ocean was the *China Clipper*. This first **commercial** airplane was called an *airboat*.

The *China Clipper* was called an airboat because it took off and landed on water.

Draw the *Spirit of St. Louis*

The *Spirit of St. Louis* was a fixed-wing plane. The wing is attached to the top of the body of the plane.

1 Choose where the horizon line and vanishing point should be. Draw the body of the plane, with the lines leading to the vanishing point. Add the wings.

Horizon

Vanishing Point

2 Add the tail and the supports of the wings.

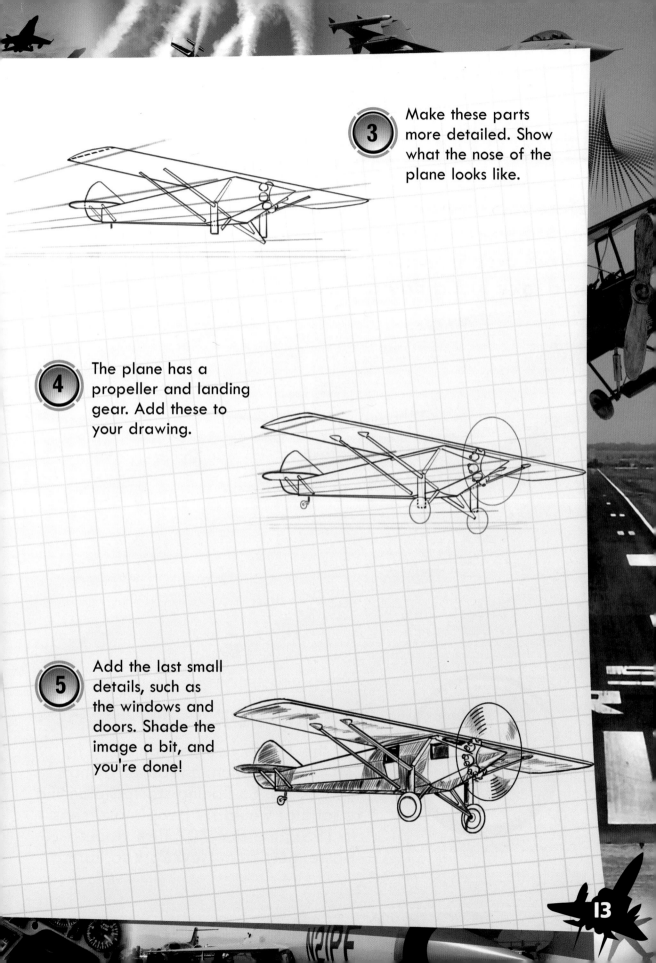

3 Make these parts more detailed. Show what the nose of the plane looks like.

4 The plane has a propeller and landing gear. Add these to your drawing.

5 Add the last small details, such as the windows and doors. Shade the image a bit, and you're done!

Modern Aircraft

Before the *China Clipper*, people would have to sail for days and weeks to cross oceans. Now they knew it could take just a day or two.

Passenger jets were new in the 1950s, but very common in the skies today!

Boeing 707

By the 1950s people wanted to fly off on a vacation instead of flying into battle. So Boeing started planning a jet that would fly people overseas. In 1958, the first 707 flew about 100 passengers from New York to Paris.

Boeing 747

Now that planes could fly large numbers of people, even more people wanted to fly. Boeing designed the first 747 jumbo jet in 1966. By 1970, the 747 flew over a million passengers. These jumbo jets carry 500 passengers at once. Boeing still makes 747s today to carry both people and **freight**.

Northrop Grumman B-2

Countries still depend on airplanes for protection. Northrop-Grumman built the B-2. It can fly 6,000 miles (9,656 kilometers) on one tank of fuel and hit a target in any kind of weather. The B-2 performs **reconnaissance**, too.

Lockheed SR-71 Blackbird

Commercial aircraft are not the only kind of modern planes. Governments use planes for **surveillance**. The U.S. started using the Lockheed SR-71 for spying in 1966. The plane was designed so well that the U.S. used it through the 1980s. The plane still holds records for speed and **altitude**.

The B-2 has a very different design from a commercial airplane.

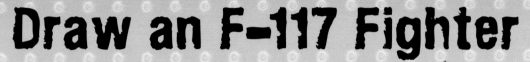

Draw an F-117 Fighter

The F-117 could fly and attack without being noticed by enemy radar.

Vanishing Point

Horizon

1 Where is the vanishing point on the horizon? Draw the outline of the F-117, but angle it so it follows the lines that lead to the vanishing point.

2 Draw more of the body of the plane. Which lines should lead to the vanishing point?

16

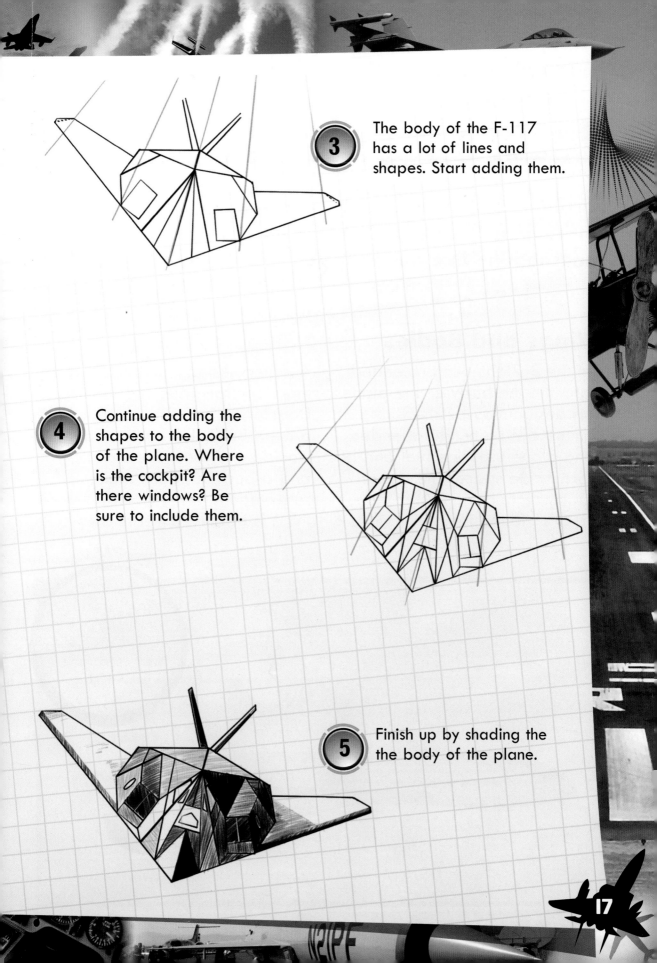

3 The body of the F-117 has a lot of lines and shapes. Start adding them.

4 Continue adding the shapes to the body of the plane. Where is the cockpit? Are there windows? Be sure to include them.

5 Finish up by shading the the body of the plane.

Future Airplanes

Airplane designs are always changing and improving. The planes your children fly in may look nothing like the ones you see today.

Wings and Bodies

On the B-2, the wings blended right into the body of the plane. This design may be the future of commercial flight. This blended wing plane uses less fuel and has more inside space. The design can fly higher and faster than today's planes, too.

Another design could make flying more comfortable. The Stratos Double-Decker airplane has a huge body. Each passenger would have room for a chair and a bed. But don't make reservations yet. The real thing is about 20 years away.

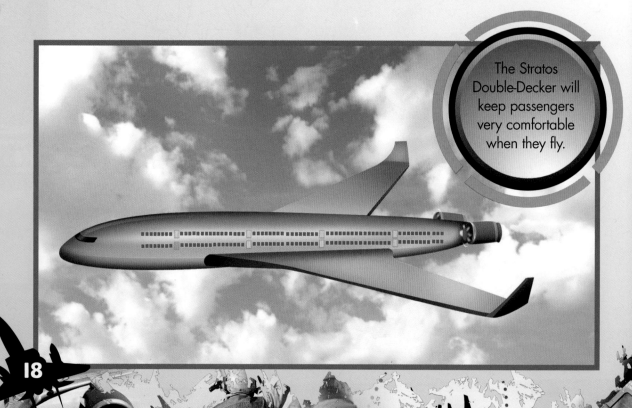

The Stratos Double-Decker will keep passengers very comfortable when they fly.

Solar Planes

Airplane fuel costs money, but solar power is free. Scientists hope planes can use solar power. A plane would need many solar collectors. This would make the wings very wide. Planes flying at night would not have the Sun for power. So designers must find a way to store energy when it isn't available.

Personal Aircraft

Many people hate flying. Sitting close to strangers, rushing through airports, and waiting in lines is not fun. Engineers are exploring the idea of airplanes as small as a car. These personal airplanes can fly whenever and wherever a person would need to go.

Someday, you may park a plane in your driveway next to your car!

Draw a Futuristic Airplane

Airplanes of the future might have solar panels or unusual engines.

Vanishing Point

Horizon

1 As before, start with a vanishing point on the horizon. Draw the body of the plane to follow the lines to the vanishing point. Add a line where the wings will go.

2 Fill out the shape of the body and each of the wings. Notice the ends of the wings follow the lines to the vanishing point.

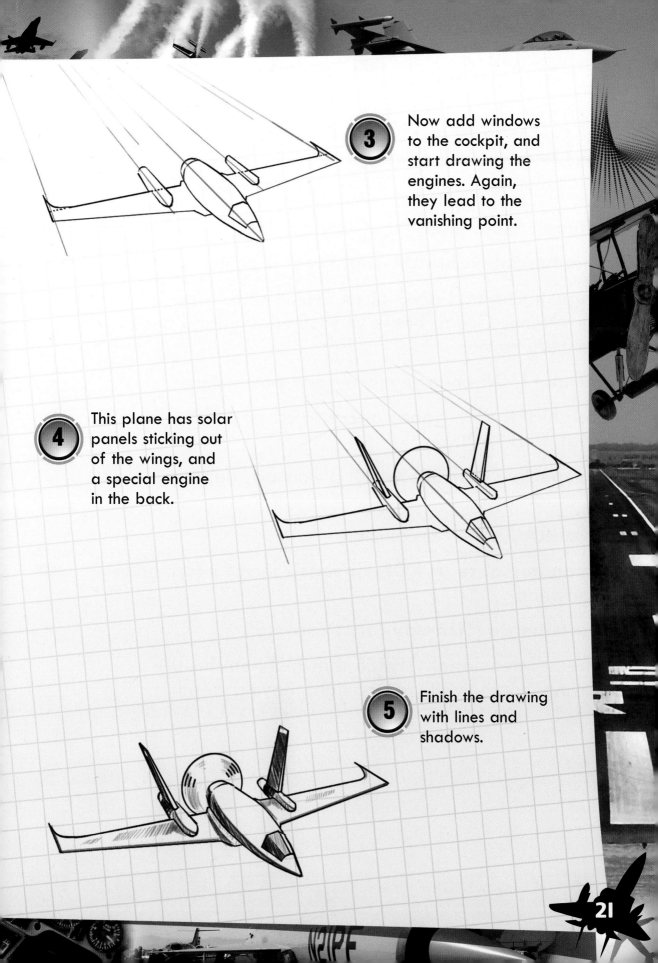

3 Now add windows to the cockpit, and start drawing the engines. Again, they lead to the vanishing point.

4 This plane has solar panels sticking out of the wings, and a special engine in the back.

5 Finish the drawing with lines and shadows.

Glossary

altitude (AL-ti-tood): how high an object is in the air

commercial (kuh-MUR-shuhl): for business

English Channel (ING-glish CHAN-uhl): a part of the Atlantic Ocean between southern England and northern France

fortune (FOR-chuhn): money and possessions

freight (FRAYT): goods or cargo carried by a plane, boat, truck, or train

perspective (pur-SPEK-tiv): giving art, depth, or distance

rare (RAIR): very uncommon

reconnaissance (ri-KON-ni-sens): secret information-gathering

surveillance (SUR-vay-lanss): spying

three-dimensional (THREE duh-MEN-shuhn-ul): having length, width, and height; having depth

Index

Websites

http://www.nasm.si.edu/wrightbrothers/
A website about a museum devoted to the Wright Brothers.

http://www.space.com/technology/top10_warplanes_history.html
A website which contains a list of the top ten war aircraft in history.

http://www.americaslibrary.gov/cgi-bin/page.cgi/aa/earhart
The Library of Congress website covering the life and adventures of
Amelia Earhart.

www.dirjournal.com/kids/arts/drawing/
A website with stories, art, and comparisons.

http://science.howstuffworks.com/classic-airplanes.htm
A website devoted to explaining airplanes the Wright Brothers'
invention to modern aircraft.

http://quest.arc.nasa.gov/aero/background/
NASA's educational website about how airplanes fly.

About the Author
Ann Becker is an avid reader. Ann likes to read books, magazines,
and even Internet articles. She hopes that someday she will get
to go on a game show and put all of that reading to good use!

About the Illustrator
Maria Menon has been illustrating children's books for almost
a decade. She loves making illustrations of animals, especially
dragons and dinosaurs. She is fond of pets and has two dogs
named Spot and Lara. When she is not busy illustrating, Maria
spends her time watching animated movies.